Peter Pan

J. M. **Barrie**

Illustrated by **Alida Massari**
Adapted by **Gina D. B. Clemen**

Series editor: Robert Hill
Editor: Elena Tonus
Design and art direction: Nadia Maestri
Computer graphics: Carlo Cibrario-Sent, Simona Corniola
Picture research: Alice Graziotin

© 2014 Black Cat

First edition: January 2014

Picture credits:
Istockphoto; Dreams Time; Shutterstock Images; Rue des Archives/Tips Images: 5;
© RobertHarding/Cuboimages : 13t; DeAgostini Pictures Library: 13b; Adam Woolfitt/
Cuboimages: 14r; © WALT DISNEY PICTURES/WebPhoto: 29; © Bettmann/CORBIS:
44t; Peter Macdiarmid/Getty Images: 44b; © English Heritage/Arcaid/Corbis: 59;
© Peter Aprahamian/CORBIS: 60; © WALT DISNEY PICTURES/WebPhoto: 61l;
© COLUMBIA PICTURES/WebPhoto: 61c; © BUENA VISTA/WebPhoto: 61r.

We would be happy to receive your comments and suggestions, and give
you any other information concerning
our material.
info@blackcat-cideb.com
blackcat-cideb.com

Member of CISQ Federation

RINA
ISO 9001:2008
Certified Quality System

The design, production and distribution of educational materials
for the Black Cat brand are managed in compliance with the rules of
Quality Management System which fulfils the requirements of the
standard ISO 9001 (Rina Cert. No. 24298/02/S - IQNet Reg. No. IT-80096)

ISBN   978-88-530-1413-9   Book + audio CD

Printed in Croatia by Grafički zavod Hrvatske d.o.o., Zagreb

Contents

The text is recorded in full.

These symbols indicate the beginning and end of the passages linked to the listening activities.

The Characters

Back row from left: Mrs and Mr Darling; Tinker Bell; Captain Hook.
Middle row from left: Michael; John; Wendy; Peter Pan.   *Front row:* Nana and… the crocodile.

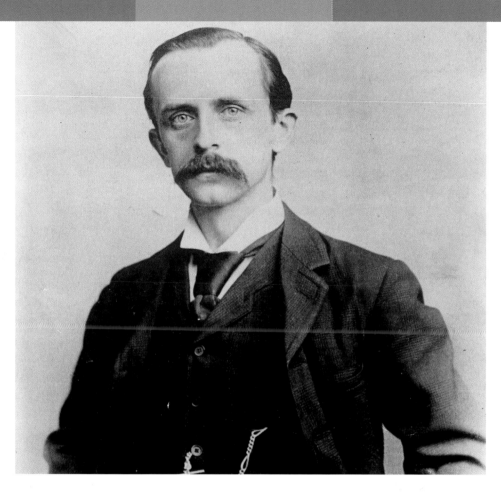

About the Author

Name: James Matthew Barrie

Born: 9 May 1860 in Kirriemuir, Scotland

Books and Plays: *The Little Minister* (1891)
                       The Little White Bird (1902)
                       Peter Pan – the play (1904)
                       Peter Pan in Kensington Gardens (a novel: 1906)
                       Peter Pan and Wendy – the novel (1911)

Awards: title of 'Sir' in 1913

Dies: June 26, 1937

BEFORE YOU READ

1 VOCABULARY
Match each word with the correct picture.

1 nursery
2 nanny
3 Newfoundland dog
4 shadow
5 kennel
6 drawer

2 LISTENING
Listen to Chapter One and decide if the sentences are true (T) or false (F).

		T	F
1	The Darling family lives in London.		
2	Wendy's brothers are called John and Michael.		
3	The three children like playing in the garden.		
4	Nana's kennel is in the garden.		
5	Mr and Mrs Darling are going to the theatre.		
6	Mrs Darling puts the boy's shadow in her pocket.		

3 READING PICTURES
Look at the picture on page 9 and answer the questions.

1 How many objects can you count in the picture?
2 Can you name them?
3 Who are those people?

CHAPTER ONE

The Darling Family

Wendy, John and Michael Darling live in a big house in London. It is a lovely house with a lot of rooms and a garden outside. They live with their parents, Mr and Mrs Darling. The Darlings are a happy family.

Mr and Mrs Darling love their children very much.

Wendy is the first child and she is pretty. She has got long blond hair and blue eyes. John is the second child and he is tall and thin. He has got brown hair and brown eyes and he wears glasses. Michael is the third child and he has got brown hair and blue eyes. The three children are very friendly.

Wendy, John and Michael like playing in the nursery. It is a big, sunny nursery and there are pictures on the walls. There are a lot of toys in the nursery.

The children have a nanny called Nana – she is a big Newfoundland dog.[1] She is a wonderful nanny and looks after the children.

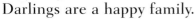

She loves them and they love her.

Her kennel is in the nursery.

One evening Mr and Mrs Darling put on some very nice clothes. They are going to a dinner party with their friends. Mrs Darling goes to the nursery. The children are playing happily.

Wendy sees her mother and says, 'What a lovely dress!'

'Yes,' says John, 'you're wearing a beautiful dress.'

'Thank you', says Mrs Darling. 'Your father and I are going to a dinner party this evening.'

Then she looks at Nana and says, 'Nana, it's almost half past eight. It's time to put the children to bed.'

Nana looks at Mrs Darling with her big brown eyes and barks. [1] She goes to the bathroom and turns on the hot water for Michael's bath. But Michael does not like having baths.

'No,' says little Michael, 'I don't want to have a bath! And I don't want to go to bed!'

Nana is a good nanny and the children must listen to her. Michael has his bath.

Then she gives the children their pajamas and they are ready for bed now.

Mrs Darling comes to the nursery again and smiles. 'Good work, Nana! The children are ready for bed.'

Nana looks at Mrs Darling and barks. Then she goes and sits near her kennel.

'I can hear a noise outside the window,' says Wendy.

'Yes,' says John, 'I can hear it too.'

Mrs Darling goes to the nursery window and is very surprised. She sees a young boy outside the nursery window. Nana barks loudly and

1. **Barks :**

shuts the window quickly. The boy's shadow falls on the floor and the young boy flies away.

'Who's there?' asks Mrs Darling. She opens the window and looks outside, but she can't see anything. 'How strange! There's no one here.'

She turns around and sees the boy's shadow on the floor. Wendy, John and Michael see it too.

'What's that?' they ask, looking at the shadow on the floor.

'It's the poor boy's shadow,' says Mrs Darling.

'What can we do with it?' asks Wendy.

'Let's put it in the drawer,' says Mrs Darling.

The children get into bed.

Mr Darling takes Nana to the garden.

Then he goes to the sitting room and waits for Mrs Darling.

Mrs Darling sings to Wendy, John and Michael, and kisses them. She is a wonderful mother.

Soon the three children are sleeping.

Mr and Mrs Darling go to their bedroom. They put on their coats and go to the dinner party.

UNDERSTANDING THE TEXT

1 **COMPREHENSION CHECK**

Read these sentences about Chapter One and choose the correct answer – A, B or C. There is an example at the beginning (0).

0   Wendy is the first child and
   A ☐ she is 12 years old.
   B ☐ she does not like having baths.
   C ☑ she is pretty.

1   John is the second child and
   A ☐ he is unfriendly.
   B ☐ he wears glasses.
   C ☐ he is short.

2   Michael is the third child and
   A ☐ he is tall and thin.
   B ☐ he has got blond hair.
   C ☐ he does not like having baths.

3   Mrs Darling is wearing
   A ☐ a beautiful dress.
   B ☐ a new coat.
   C ☐ a beautiful hat.

4   Mrs Darling goes to the nursery window
   A ☐ and sees a young boy.
   B ☐ and sees a fairy.
   C ☐ and looks at the lights of the city.

5   Mr Darling takes Nana
   A ☐ to the bathroom.
   B ☐ to the sitting room.
   C ☐ to the garden.

6   When the three children are sleeping
   A ☐ Mr and Mrs Darling go to bed.
   B ☐ Mr and Mrs Darling go to a dinner party.
   C ☐ Mr and Mrs Darling have dinner in their bedroom.

2 OPPOSITES

A Match each adjective (1-6) with its opposite (A-F).

1 ☐ tall
2 ☐ happy
3 ☐ good
4 ☐ hot
5 ☐ friendly
6 ☐ open

A sad
B bad
C shut
D short
E cold
F unfriendly

B Now write six sentences using the adjectives above.

3 THE FIVE SENSES

**A 'I can *hear* a noise outside the window,' says Wendy.
Do you know the five senses? Complete the sentences (1-5) with their endings (A-E).**

1 ☐ You hear with…
2 ☐ You see with…
3 ☐ You smell with…
4 ☐ You taste with…
5 ☐ You feel with…

A your hands and fingers.
B your nose.
C your ears.
D your eyes.
E your mouth.

B Speaking – We use our senses all the time. Work with a partner and use these ideas to help you.

1 Describe your classroom.
2 Describe your teacher.
3 When you go to the park what can you see?
4 When you walk down a busy street, what can you hear?

T : GRADE 2

4 SPEAKING – ROOMS IN THE HOME

Wendy, John and Michael live in a big house with a nice garden. Draw a plan of your house and tell your partner about it. Use these questions to help you.

- What is your house like?
- How many rooms has it got?

- What is your bedroom like?
- What is your favourite room?

Tower Bridge.

London

Great Britain

The story you are reading starts in London in the early 1900s. London is a wonderful city and it is the capital of the United Kingdom. Today almost 8 million people live there.

London is a very green city. There are more than 300 parks! Hyde Park is a very big park with more than 4,000 trees. You can go biking in the park, or you can ride a boat on The Serpentine Lake. In the summer there are music concerts in the park.

In Kensington Gardens there is a statue of Peter Pan and a lot of visitors go and see it.

The statue of Peter Pan

Big Ben.   Along the banks of the River Thames.

The River Thames runs through the city and a lot of bridges [1] cross it. You can take a lovely boat ride on the River Thames and ride under Tower Bridge.

Big Ben is the name of an enormous [2] clock on top of a tall tower. You can see the tower and the clock next to the Houses of Parliament, on the River Thames.

The Tower of London is a very old tower, it was built between 1070 and 1100. You can visit the Tower and see the Queen's crown jewels. [3]

There are always a lot of interesting things to do and see in London. There are more than 240 important museums and many of them are free. There are also a lot of important theatres.

1 **COMPREHENSION CHECK**
Answer these questions.

1   How many people live in London today?
2   How many parks are there in London?
3   Where can you see a statue of Peter Pan?
4   What river runs through London?
5   What is Big Ben?
6   How many museums are there in London?

1. **Bridge** :

2. **Enormous** : very big.   3. **Crown jewels** :

14

CHAPTER TWO

Peter's Shadow

verything is dark and silent in the nursery. Wendy, John and Michael are sleeping and dreaming. Outside the nursery window there is a small ball of light. The nursery window is open. Suddenly the small ball of light comes into the nursery through the window and flies around. It is a fairy called Tinker Bell. She is very small and lovely. She is looking for something inside the nursery.

After a moment a young boy comes into the nursery through the open window and looks around.

'Tink,' he says, 'where are you? Where's my shadow? Please, find it.'

Tinker Bell flies around the nursery and stops near a drawer. She opens it carefully and finds his shadow. Then she gives it to him.

'Thank you, Tink!' says the boy happily. He goes to the bathroom and gets some soap. 'Now I can put the shadow on my feet with some soap.' He tries to stick it on his feet but he can't.

'Why can't I put my shadow on my feet?' he thinks. 'Now I haven't got a shadow.' He is very sad and starts to cry.

Wendy hears the boy crying and she wakes up. She sees a young boy, but she is not afraid. He has got red hair and a friendly face. His clothes are made of green leaves. She thinks, 'What's this boy doing in the nursery?'

'Little boy, why are you crying?' Wendy asks.

The boy smiles and asks, 'What's your name?'

'My name's Wendy Moira Angela Darling. And what's yours?'

'Peter Pan.'

'Is that all?' asks Wendy, looking at him.

'Yes, that's all,' says Peter. Then he thinks, 'My name is very short!'

Wendy looks at his shadow on the floor and says, 'Is this your shadow?'

'Yes,' says Peter, 'but I can't put it on.'

Wendy smiles and says, 'I can sew it on.'

'Can you? Oh, please, do it!' says Peter happily.

Wendy gets her big sewing basket [1] and sews on Peter's shadow carefully. Peter looks at her and is very glad. After a few minutes Wendy says, 'I've finished! Now you've got your shadow again.'

Peter looks at the floor and he can see his shadow. He is happy and he dances around the nursery.

'Thank you, Wendy!' he says. 'You're a wonderful girl!'

'Do you really think so?' asks Wendy.

'Yes, I do,' says Peter, looking at Wendy.

Wendy smiles and gives Peter a kiss on the cheek.

'Oh!' says Peter. 'That's nice.'

1. **Sewing basket :**

'How old are you Peter?' asks Wendy.

Peter thinks for a moment and says, 'I don't know. But I'm young, and I don't want to grow up. I don't want to become an adult. I want to be a boy forever and have lots of fun!'

Wendy listens to Peter and is surprised. Then Peter looks for his fairy. Suddenly he hears a noise and looks in a drawer. Little Tinker Bell flies out. Wendy is happy to see a fairy, but Tinker Bell is afraid. She hides behind the big clock.

'Where do you live, Peter?' asks Wendy.

'I sometimes live in Kensington Gardens,'[2] says Peter, 'but most of the time I live in Neverland with the Lost Boys.'

Wendy does not understand. 'Neverland? The Lost Boys? Who are they?'

'The Lost Boys haven't got a mother or father,' says Peter. 'They're alone in the world and they live in Neverland. I'm their Captain.'

'Neverland sounds like a wonderful place!' says Wendy.

'It is,' says Peter, 'and we have lots of fun there. In Neverland we fight the pirates. We swim in the lagoon with beautiful mermaids. A lot of lovely fairies live in the trees in the forest. They're my friends.'

'What fun!' says Wendy.

'Well, I must go back to Neverland now,' says Peter. 'I must tell the Lost Boys a story. You know, they love stories.'

'I know a lot of stories,' says Wendy.

'Then come with me to Neverland!' says Peter. 'You can tell us lots of stories. And you can see the beautiful mermaids in the lagoon. Come with me! We all want a mother.'

'Oh, I can't come with you,' says Wendy. 'I can't fly.'

'I can teach you to fly,' says Peter. 'It's very easy.'

2. **Kensington Gardens** : a beautiful park in London (see dossier on pages 13-14).

Peter's Shadow

'Can you teach John and Michael to fly, too?' asks Wendy.

'Of course!' says Peter.

Wendy goes to John and Michael and says, 'Wake up! Quickly! Peter Pan is here. He's from Neverland. It's a fun place!'

John and Michael wake up, and they are very surprised.

'We can go to Neverland with him,' says Wendy. 'But we must learn to fly.'

'That's difficult,' says John.

'No, it's not,' says Peter. 'Look at me!' Peter flies around the nursery and the children look at him. They are excited and try to fly, but they fall on the beds and on the floor.

'It's impossible!' they say.

'You need some fairy dust,' says Peter, laughing. He puts some fairy dust on their heads. 'Now try again.'

Wendy, John and Michael can fly now and they are very happy.

'Look, I can fly!' says Wendy.

'We can, too!' say John and Michael.

'Now we can go to Neverland with Peter,' says Wendy happily.

'Tink,' says Peter, 'show us the way to Neverland!'

They follow Tinker Bell and fly out of the nursery window. There are a lot of stars in the night sky. In the garden Nana looks at the sky and barks loudly. Mr and Mrs Darling return from the dinner party at eleven o'clock. They go to the nursery, but it is empty! Where are the children?

UNDERSTANDING THE TEXT

1 COMPREHENSION CHECK
Are these sentences 'Right' (A) or 'Wrong' (B)? If there is not enough
information to answer (A) or (B), choose 'Doesn't say' (C). There is an
example at the beginning (0).

		A	B	C
0	Tinker Bell comes into the Darling nursery at ten o'clock.			✓
1	Peter Pan and Tinker Bell are looking for Peter's shadow.			
2	Tinker Bell finds Peter's shadow under Wendy's bed.			
3	Peter wants to stick on his shadow with some soap.			
4	Wendy is afraid of Peter Pan.			
5	Tinker Bell sews on Peter's shadow.			
6	Peter Pan is twelve years old.			
7	Tinker Bell hides inside the drawer because she is afraid of Wendy.			
8	The Lost Boys haven't got a family.			
9	Fairy dust helps the three children fly to Neverland.			

T: GRADE 2

2 SPEAKING – FAMILY AND FRIENDS
Think of a member of your family. Describe him/her to your partner. Use
these questions to help you.

- What's his/her name?
- How old is he/she?
- Is he/she short or tall?
- What colour is his/her hair? And eyes?
- What clothes does he/she usually wear?

3 CHARACTERS
Look at the pictures of Wendy, John, Michael, Peter and Tinker Bell. Use
the words in the box to describe them.

> blue eyes   tall   does not want to grow up   pretty
> thin   brown hair   brown eyes   friendly   wears glasses
> long blond hair   red hair   very small   lovely
> wears clothes made of green leaves   does not like having baths

4 PREPOSITIONS

Complete each sentence with the correct preposition from the box.

> under   on   behind   in   for   inside   at   outside

1 Peter's shadow is .... the drawer.
2 There is a ball of light .... the nursery window.
3 Nana is sitting in the garden .... a tree.
4 John is sleeping .... his bed.
5 The dinner party is .... Saturday.
6 The children have lunch .... 12.30.
7 Peter Pan is hiding .... the door.
8 'Here's a toy .... you, Michael,' says Mrs Darling.

WHERE DO YOU LIVE, PETER? WHAT'S YOUR NAME?

Where and *what* are question words.
Here are some words we often use to make questions.
What...? (for things)   *Where*...? (for places)
Who...? (for people)   *Why*...? (for a reason)
When...? (for time)

5 QUESTION WORDS

Read the sentences below and write the correct question word. There is an example at the beginning (0).

0 ......Why........ is Tinker Bell in the nursery?
   She is in the nursery because she is looking for Peter's shadow.

1 .... is the nanny in the Darling family?
   Nana is the nanny in the Darling family.

2 .... is in the drawer?
   Peter's shadow is in the drawer.

3 .... does Peter Pan live?
   He lives in Neverland.

4 .... do the Darling children go to bed?
   They go to bed at half past eight.

5 .... is Peter crying?
   Peter is crying because he hasn't got a shadow.

6 .... are Mr and Mrs Darling going?
   They are going to a dinner party.

BEFORE YOU READ

1 **VOCABULARY**
Match each word with the correct picture.

1	beard	**3**	crocodile	**5**	bow and arrow
2	hook	**4**	alarm clock	**6**	Indian chief

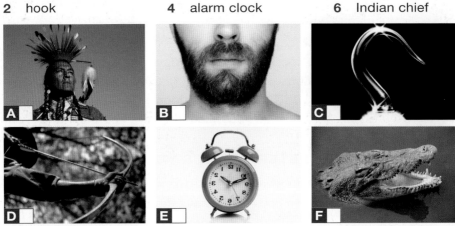

2 **LISTENING**
**Listen to the first part of Chapter Three and choose the correct answer –
A, B or C.**

1 Where do the Lost Boys live?
- A ☐ In an underground home.
- B ☐ In the lagoon.
- C ☐ On the *Jolly Roger*.

2 How many Lost Boys are there?
- A ☐ five
- B ☐ two
- C ☐ six

3 Who is not afraid of the pirates?
- A ☐ Tootles
- B ☐ Nibs
- C ☐ Curly

4 What is the *Jolly Roger*?
- A ☐ A pirate ship.
- B ☐ The name of the underground home.
- C ☐ The name of the crocodile.

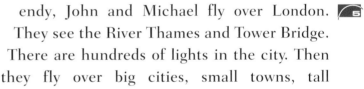

CHAPTER THREE

Neverland*

Wendy, John and Michael fly over London. They see the River Thames and Tower Bridge. There are hundreds of lights in the city. Then they fly over big cities, small towns, tall mountains, green forests and blue seas. At last they see an island in the sea below them. It is a beautiful island.

'That's Neverland,' says Peter, looking down at the island. It is a sunny day now but it's windy.

'Neverland!' say the children happily.

'Look, John,' says Wendy, 'there's the lagoon.'

'And there's the big forest,' says Michael. The children are excited.

The Lost Boys live in the green forest in a secret underground home. There are six Lost Boys and their names are: Curly, Nibs, Tootles, Slightly Soiled [1] and the Twins. They are waiting for Peter in the underground home.

---

*(see the map of Neverland at the end of the book).

1. **Slightly Soiled** : this name means 'a little dirty'.

Suddenly they hear the voices of the pirates.

'I can hear the pirates!' says Tootles. 'They're in the forest.'

'I'm afraid of them,' says Slightly Soiled.

'What can we do?' asks Curly.

'I'm not afraid of the pirates,' says Nibs. He goes out of the underground home. He hides behind a big tree and looks around. He sees the terrible pirates. They are walking in the forest and they are big and strong. They live on a pirate ship called the *Jolly Roger*.

The pirates' captain is James Hook. He is a very bad pirate. He has got black eyes, black hair and a big black beard. He hates Peter Pan. He has got only one hand the other hand is a hook! In the past Peter cut [2] off Captain Hook's right arm during a fight. A crocodile ate [3] the arm because crocodiles are always hungry. Now the crocodile follows Captain Hook everywhere because he wants to eat him. The crocodile has an alarm clock in its stomach! Captain Hook can always hear it.

'We must find Peter Pan and the Lost Boys,' says Captain Hook angrily. 'I know they live in this forest! *But where?*'

The pirates look everywhere but they cannot find the secret underground home.

Suddenly Captain Hook hears the alarm clock, 'Tick, tock, tick, tock!'

'The crocodile is near!' cries Captain Hook. 'He wants to eat me! We must leave the forest quickly!' He runs away and the pirates follow him.

Soon some American Indians come to the forest. They walk silently and carry bows and arrows. They are looking for the pirates. The pirates are their enemies. [4] Their leader is Tiger Lily. She is the lovely daughter of the American Indian chief. She likes Peter Pan a lot. The Indians cannot find the Pirates and they soon go away. Now the Lost

2. **Cut** : the Past Simple of the verb 'to cut'.
3. **Ate** : the Past Simple of the verb 'to eat'.
4. **Enemies** : opposite of friends (the singular is 'enemy').

Boys can leave the underground home and play in the forest.

Nibs looks at the sky and says, 'Look, there's a white bird in the sky.'

The Lost Boys look at the sky and Curly asks, 'Is it really a bird?'

'Of course it's a bird,' says Tinker Bell. 'It's a Wendy bird. You must shoot[5] it!' Sometimes Tinker Bell is a bad fairy. She knows that it is Wendy, but she doesn't like her.

Nibs takes his bow and arrow and looks at the sky. He shoots Wendy and she falls to the ground. Then the Lost Boys go and see Wendy.

'She's not a bird!' they say. 'She's a lovely girl.'

Peter flies down with John and Michael and asks, 'Where's Wendy?'

Tootles says, 'Here she is.'

Peter goes to her and asks, 'Wendy, are you alright?'

Wendy slowly opens her eyes and smiles at Peter.

'Yes, I'm alright,' she says, 'I'm lucky because the arrow hit the button of my nightdress.'

The Lost Boys are very sorry.

'Poor Wendy!' says Curly. 'What can we do?'

'I've got a good idea,' says Slightly Soiled. 'We can build her a little house'.

When the little house is ready the Lost Boys go and tell Wendy.

'Come and see the little house, Wendy,' says Tootles.

'Do you like it?' ask the Lost Boys.

'Yes, I do,' says Wendy, happily. 'It's a nice little house. Thank you.'

'Wendy, can you be our mother now?' asks Nibs. 'Can you tell us bedtime stories before we go to bed?'

'Yes, please,' says Tootles, 'come and be our mother.'

'Of course,' says Wendy. 'Come in and I can tell you the story of Cinderella.'

They listen to Wendy's story and like it a lot.

5. **Shoot** : (here) hit with a bow and arrow.

UNDERSTANDING THE TEXT

1 **COMPREHENSION CHECK**

Read the summary of Chapter Three. Choose the correct option – A, B or C – for each space to say what happens in this chapter. There is an example at the beginning (0).

Wendy, John and Michael are going to Neverland. They fly (**0**) ..B... the city of London. They (**1**) .... a lot of lights in the city. Neverland is a beautiful (**2**) .... The Lost Boys wait (**3**) .... Peter Pan in the secret underground home. Tootles hears the pirates in the forest. Nibs leaves the underground home and goes to the forest. He hides (**4**) .... a big tree and looks (**5**) ....

Captain James Hook and his pirates are looking (**6**) .... Peter Pan and the Lost Boys. Captain Hook hates Peter Pan. He is afraid of the crocodile (**7**) .... It is always hungry and wants to eat (**8**) ....

Nibs sees Wendy in the sky. Tinker Bell says Wendy is a bird. Nibs takes his bow and arrow and shoots (**9**) .... She falls to the ground and he is very sorry. The Lost Boys (**10**) .... a little house for Wendy. She likes it and tells the Lost Boys bedtime stories.

0	A	up	(B)	over	C	near
1	A	watch	B	look	C	see
2	A	island	B	sea	C	lagoon
3	A	at	B	for	C	to
4	A	to	B	over	C	behind
5	A	around	B	at	C	over
6	A	to	B	by	C	for
7	A	and	B	because	C	why
8	A	him	B	he	C	it
9	A	she	B	it	C	her
10	A	do	B	build	C	get

**EVERYONE IS HAPPY.
NOW THE CROCODILE FOLLOWS CAPTAIN HOOK
EVERYWHERE BECAUSE HE WANTS TO EAT HIM.**

We use **everyone** when we talk about all people.

We use **everything** when we talk about all things.

We use **everywhere** when we talk about all places.

2 EVERYONE, EVERYTHING, EVERYWHERE
Fill in the gaps with *everyone*, *everything* or *everywhere*.

1 Captain Hook looks .... for Peter and the Lost Boys, but cannot find them.
2 .... in Neverland is beautiful.
3 Wendy makes friends with ....
4 Peter and Tinker Bell go .... together.
5 .... on the table is good to eat.
6 .... likes bedtime stories.

3 WHAT'S THE WEATHER LIKE?
Match each description (A-F) to the correct picture (1-6).

1 It's snowing.   3 It's raining.   5 It's windy.
2 It's cloudy.   4 It's sunny.   6 It's foggy.

A☐   B☐   C☐

D☐   E☐   F☐

4 CONVERSATION
Complete the five conversations. For each question (1-5), choose the correct option – A, B or C. There is an example at the beginning (0).

0 Can you speak English?
   A ☐ Yes, I know.   B ☐ Yes, I speak.   C ✓ Yes, I can.
1 Pass me the bread, please.
   A ☐ Thank you.   B ☐ Here you are.   C ☐ You're welcome.
2 Where is the bookshop?
   A ☐ I don't know.   B ☐ There isn't any.   C ☐ Five minutes.
3 Do you like school?
   A ☐ Yes, I am.   B ☐ Yes, I do.   C ☐ Yes, I can.
4 What time is dinner?
   A ☐ At six.   B ☐ Later.   C ☐ Early.
5 How many friends have you got?
   A ☐ Much.   B ☐ None.   C ☐ Any.

KEY

Fairies And Their Magic

The Blue Fairy.

People all over the world have stories about fairies and their magic. Some of these stories are very old, and some of them are called fairy tales. Fairies are part of the British, Irish, northern European and old cultures.

In *Peter Pan*, Tinker Bell is Peter's fairy. Peter says that the fairies in Neverland are his good friends.

In *Pinocchio* there is a kind fairy called the Blue Fairy. She always helps Pinocchio. In *Cinderella* a fairy godmother[1] is Cinderella's good friend.

There are fairies in one of William Shakespeare's plays, too. In *A Midsummer Night's Dream*, Oberon and Titania are the king and queen of the fairies. They live in the forest and are important characters in the play.

What some people say about fairies

They are small and have wings; they live in the forest, in trees, in flowers and in gardens; they are sometimes good and sometimes bad; they are magic; they can do good things and bad things.

1 COMPREHENSION CHECK

Are the following sentences true (T) or false (F)? Correct the false ones.

		T	F
1	Fairy tales are stories about fairies.	☐	☐
2	All fairies live in Neverland.	☐	☐
3	Some people say that fairies are magic.	☐	☐
4	Fairies always do bad things.	☐	☐
5	The Blue Fairy is Pinocchio's friend.	☐	☐
6	Shakespeare uses fairies in one of his plays.	☐	☐

1. **Fairy godmother** : (here) this fairy helps Cinderella because she does not have a mother.

CHAPTER FOUR

Danger in the Lagoon

Peter, Wendy, John, Michael and the Lost Boys often go to
the Mermaids' Lagoon. The water is blue and beautiful. They
like swimming and playing in the blue lagoon. Beautiful mermaids
live here, and they are Peter's friends. They have got long hair and
are very pretty. They play mermaid games, and then sit on Marooners'
Rock and comb their long hair. They sit in the sun and talk and laugh.

The children like the mermaids and John says, 'I want to catch a
mermaid!' He tries but the mermaid jumps into the water and swims
away. Everyone laughs.

'It's very difficult to catch a mermaid,' says Peter.

Suddenly Peter hears a noise and says, 'The pirates are coming! I
can hear them!'

John, Michael and the Lost Boys jump into the water and swim
away. They are afraid of the pirates. But Wendy stays with Peter.
They hide behind Marooners' Rock.

Danger in the Lagoon

A small boat with two pirates is coming to the lagoon. One pirate is Smee. He is old and wears glasses. The other pirate is Starkey. He is young and has got a long nose. Tiger Lily is on the boat and she is a prisoner of the pirates.

'Let's leave her on this rock,' says Smee. 'When the sea rises[1] she's going to die.' The two pirates laugh loudly. It is almost night and it is dark.

'Poor Tiger Lily!' thinks Peter. 'She is our good friend. I must save her. But what can I do?'

He thinks for a minute and then imitates[2] Captain Hook's voice. 'Cut the ropes and let Tiger Lily go! Do as I say, Smee! Let her go!'

The two pirates hear Captain Hook's voice and are very surprised. They look at each other and then they look around.

'Starkey,' says Smee, 'can you hear Hook's voice?'

'Yes,' says Starkey, looking around. 'But I don't see Hook.'

'We must listen to Hook and cut the ropes,' says Smee.

'Are you sure?' asks Starkey.

'Of course I'm sure,' says Smee.

Starkey gets a knife and cuts the ropes. Tiger Lily is free. She jumps into the water and swims away.

Captain Hook is on his ship, the *Jolly Roger*, and he sees everything. He is very angry because Tiger Lily is free.

'Peter Pan is very clever!' thinks Captain Hook. 'I must fight him.'

Captain Hook jumps into the water and swims to the rock. He fights with Peter. It is a long fight. Captain Hook hurts Peter with his big hook, but Peter does not stop fighting. He is brave.[3] At last Peter wins the fight. Captain Hook is angry and swims back to the *Jolly Roger*.

---

1. **Rises** : (here) goes up.
2. **Imitates** : copies someone's voice or actions.
3. **Brave** : not afraid.

Peter and Wendy are now alone on the rock.

'What a terrible fight, Peter!' says Wendy, looking at Peter's hand. His hand is badly hurt after the fight with Captain Hook.

'Yes,' says Peter, 'but I'm not afraid of Hook or the pirates.'

'You're a very brave boy,' says Wendy, smiling.

'Look,' says Peter, 'the sea is rising and we are in great danger here.'

'What can we do?' asks Wendy.

'We must leave this rock immediately,' says Peter, looking at the sea.

'Oh, Peter,' says Wendy, 'I can't swim or fly, because I'm very tired.'

Peter thinks for a moment.

He sees a big kite[4] with a long tail.

It is flying slowly over the lagoon.

He quickly takes the tail of the kite and says, 'Wendy, hold on to this tail and fly away with the kite.'

Wendy flies away with the kite.

'The sea is rising quickly,' Peter thinks. 'I must fly away!'

When Peter gets home, everyone is happy to see him.

4. Kite :

UNDERSTANDING THE TEXT

1 COMPREHENSION CHECK

Read these sentences and choose the correct answer – A, B or C. There is an example at the beginning (0).

0 The water at Mermaids' Lagoon is

A ☐ very cold.

B ☑ blue and beautiful.

C ☐ warm.

1 John wants to

A ☐ comb his hair.

B ☐ talk to a mermaid.

C ☐ catch a mermaid.

2 John, Michael and the Lost Boys swim away because

A ☐ they are afraid of the mermaids.

B ☐ they are afraid of the pirates.

C ☐ they are afraid of the Indians.

3 Tiger Lily is on a boat with

A ☐ Peter and Wendy.

B ☐ Smee and Starkey.

C ☐ Captain Hook and Smee.

4 Smee and Starkey hear Hook's voice

A ☐ but they don't see him.

B ☐ and they see him.

C ☐ and they talk to him.

5 Captain Hook and Peter Pan fight

A ☐ but no one wins.

B ☐ and Peter wins.

C ☐ and Captain Hook wins.

6 Peter and Wendy must leave the rock because

A ☐ Captain Hook is there.

B ☐ the sea is rising.

C ☐ it is late.

2 VOCABULARY

A Read these definitions. What is the word for each one? The first letter is already there. There is one space for each other letter of the word. There is an example at the beginning (0).

0 This person looks after children: n a n n y

1 The Darling family lives here: L _ _ _ _ _

2 This wakes you up in the morning: a _ _ _ _ c _ _ _ _

3 A dog lives in it: k _ _ _ _ _

4 You keep things inside it: d _ _ _ _ _

5 They help you to see well: g _ _ _ _ _ _

B Now find the words in the word square and circle them.

```
B F D V K E N N E L A C J R
A N G P U B I H T B D G E B
S O O L O N D O N P O W X Y
W B I K A Z J T S V A Z B O
T R J L R S L V A R N M U E
O I K C M Y S H D H O N B D
E D R E O O M E B N A N N Y
R G U I D M P E S O V I S P
X E T O V G B L M B A S O W
A M I A L A R M C L O C K S
C Z E U P H W C N F U T V N
```

T: GRADE 1

3 SPEAKING – CLOTHES

Peter Pan wears clothes made of leaves. What do you like to wear? Work with a partner and use these questions to help you.

- Describe the clothes your partner is wearing.
- What are your favourite clothes?
- Do you buy clothes with your friends or with your parents?
- What are your favourite colours?

KEY

4 NOTICES

Which notice (A-H) says this? There is an example at the beginning (0).

A

A LONDON PUBLIC LIBRARY

Silence Please - No food or drink inside

B

Kensington Gardens

Open all year

No ball games

C

Sir Richard's Pet Shop

We sell only dogs and kennels.

D

London City Centre

Pedestrian Zone

No cars or bikes

E

Westminster Hotel and Restaurant

Guests always welcome! We never close!

F

Marie's French Bakery
Open every morning
7-noon
Chocolate cake on
Sundays

G

NEVERLAND POST OFFICE

Open every day except Sunday.

H

Tower of London

Famous Historical Site
Open weekday
mornings only.

0 You can't play football here. ....B....

1 You can always come here. ....

2 You can't buy a bird here. ....

3 You can buy stamps here on Wednesday. ....

4 You can't buy bread here in the afternoon. ....

5 You must not eat in here. ....

5 READING A MAP

A Can you read a map? Look at the map of Neverland at the end of the book and answer the questions. Tick the correct answer.

1   Wendy and Peter are on Marooners' Rock. They want to go to the underground home. They must go
    A ☐ west   B ☐ south   C ☐ east

2   Nibs is at Kidd's Creek. He wants to go to Slightly Gulch. He must go
    A ☐ north   B ☐ west   C ☐ south

3   John and Michael are at Slightly Gulch. They want to go to the Mermaids' Lagoon. They must go
    A ☐ south   B ☐ east   C ☐ north

4   Tiger Lily is in the Indian camp. She wants to go to the Mysterious River. She must go
    A ☐ west   B ☐ east   C ☐ south

5   The Lost Boys are in the underground home. They want to go to Kidd's Creek. They must go
    A ☐ north   B ☐ west   C ☐ south

6   Captain Hook is on Marooners' Rock. He wants to go to the Indian Camp. He must go
    A ☐ east   B ☐ west   C ☐ north

B Now work with your partner and draw a map of your own secret island. Give it an exciting name. Put mountains, rivers, lagoons, forests, beaches and deserts on your map. Remember to put North, South, East and West on your map. Is there a secret underground home? Show your map to the class and ask questions like those in exercise 5 A.

BEFORE YOU READ

1 LISTENING

Listen to the first part of Chapter Five and circle the correct word.

1   The underground home is a *safe/dangerous* place.
2   Everyone sits in front of the fireplace *before/after* dinner.
3   Neverland is *a boring/an exciting* place.
4   Wendy *sometimes/never* thinks about her parents.
5   Wendy tells a new bedtime story about *two pirates/two parents*.

A Secret Place

he underground home is a secret place in the big forest. It is a safe place because no one knows where it is. There is only one big room with a fireplace.[1] It is a happy, warm home.

Wendy, John and Michael are very happy there. Wendy is a wonderful mother. She cooks and sews for everyone. Every evening after dinner, everyone sits in front of the fireplace. Wendy tells great bedtime stories. The Lost Boys love these stories and are happy because they finally have a mother. John and Michael are happy because there is an exciting adventure every day. They are never bored.

Peter Pan is the perfect father. He brings home food and protects[2] his family. He and Wendy play games with the children and laugh with them. Everyone is having a wonderful time.

But in London, Mr and Mrs Darling are not happy. They are very sad because they can't find their three children. And Nana is sad, too.

'Where are our three children?' they think.

1. **Fireplace** :   2. **Protects** : keeps them safe.

A Secret Place

Wendy sometimes thinks about her parents.

One evening she says, 'This evening I'm going to tell you a new bedtime story. It takes place in England.' Everyone sits down in front of the fireplace and listens to her.

'In the city of London there are two parents. They're very sad because they can't find their three children. Every night they leave the nursery window open. They want their children to return. They wait and wait, but their three children don't return. These poor parents are terribly sad...'

'But Wendy,' say John and Michael, 'that's the story of our parents.'

Peter listens to the story and says, 'Sometimes parents forget their children and other children take their place.'

Wendy, John and Michael are surprised. They look at Peter.

'Are you sure, Peter?' asks Wendy.

'Yes, I'm sure,' says Peter.

'Perhaps there are other children in our nursery and in our beds!' says Wendy. 'John, Michael, we must go home immediately!'

John and Michael look at Wendy and say, 'Do we *really* have to go?'

'Yes, we must go home,' says Wendy. 'Quickly! We haven't got much time!'

'But we're happy here in Neverland with Peter and the Lost Boys,' says John.

'There's a new adventure every day,' says Michael.

'And we're never bored,' says John. 'Neverland is a wonderful place!'

'Oh, Wendy,' say the Lost Boys, 'please don't go away. Don't leave us!'

Wendy looks at the Lost Boys and says, 'Please, don't be sad. You can come to London and live with us! You can be part of the Darling family.'

'Oh, Wendy,' say the Lost Boys, 'thank you! That's wonderful! We can have a real family in London.'

Nibs and Tootles jump up and down and laugh. The other Lost Boys dance around the room. They are very happy.

Peter is not happy. 'I'm not coming with you to London.'

Everyone is surprised and looks at him.

'Why?' asks Wendy.

'I don't want to grow up,' says Peter. 'I don't want to become an adult. I want to be a boy forever.'

'But Peter,' says Wendy, 'all boys and girls grow up. They become adults.'

'No!' says Peter angrily. 'I don't want to grow up! You can go, but I'm not coming.' He turns around and looks at the wall.

Wendy, John, Michael and the Lost Boys say goodbye to Peter, and leave the underground Home. They start to walk in the forest. But they don't know that the pirates are hiding behind the trees. They are waiting for them.

Suddenly the pirates jump out of the forest. The children are very surprised and try to run away. But there are a lot of pirates and they take the children to the *Jolly Roger*.

Peter is inside the underground home and he does not hear anything. He sits in front of the fireplace and thinks about Wendy, John and Michael and the Lost Boys. He is sad without them.

'Tap, tap, tap!' There is someone at the door.

Peter goes to the door and asks, 'Who's there?'

He hears the sound of little bells and opens the door. Tinker Bell flies in and says, 'The children are with the pirates!'

'What do you mean, Tink?' asks Peter.

'Wendy, John, Michael and the Lost Boys are on the *Jolly Roger* with Captain Hook!' says Tinker Bell. 'They're in danger!'

'Oh, no!' says Peter. 'We must save them. Let's go to the *Jolly Roger*, quickly! I want to fight Hook!'

Peter and Tinker Bell leave the underground home and fly to the *Jolly Roger*.

UNDERSTANDING THE TEXT

1 **COMPREHENSION CHECK**
Are these sentences 'Right' (A) or 'Wrong' (B)? If there is not enough information to answer (A) or (B), choose 'Doesn't say' (C). There is an example at the beginning (0).

		A	B	C
0	Tinker Bell lives in the underground home.	✓		
1	There are three big rooms in the underground home.			
2	Wendy cooks dinner at six o'clock.			
3	John and Michael have a lot of fun every day.			
4	Mr and Mrs Darling always close the nursery window at night.			
5	Wendy tells a funny bedtime story that takes place in Neverland.			
6	Wendy never thinks about her parents.			
7	Wendy decides to go home immediately.			
8	Peter Pan stays in Neverland because he does not want to grow up.			
9	Captain Hook takes the children to the *Jolly Roger*.			
10	Peter Pan and Tinker Bell want to save the children.			

'I DON'T WANT TO BECOME AN ADULT,' SAYS PETER. PETER PAN DOESN'T LIVE IN LONDON, HE LIVES IN NEVERLAND.

We form the negative of the Present Simple of most verbs by using **don't** (**do not**) and **doesn't** (**does not**).

I/you/we/they **don't live**

He/she/it **doesn't live**

2 **PRESENT SIMPLE NEGATIVE**
Complete these sentences using the verb in brackets. Decide if the sentence is positive or negative and add *don't* or *doesn't* when necessary. There is an example at the beginning (0).

0   Peter ...<u>doesn't want</u>.... (*want*) to go to London.
1   Michael .... (*like*) having baths.
2   Wendy .... (*tell*) wonderful bedtime stories.
3   The Darling children .... (*go*) to school during the summer.
4   The pirates .... (*know*) where the underground home is.
5   John .... (*wear*) glasses.
6   Wendy .... (*cook*) dinner for the Lost Boys.

3 VOCABULARY – ODD ONE OUT

A Circle the word in each group that is different from the others.

	A		B		C		D	
1	A	sitting room	B	kitchen	C	nursery	D	fireplace
2	A	England	B	Italy	C	London	D	Turkey
3	A	party	B	breakfast	C	lunch	D	dinner
4	A	tall	B	short	C	thin	D	sad
5	A	dress	B	shoes	C	coat	D	jacket
6	A	hair	B	eyes	C	nose	D	ears

B Now complete the sentences with the odd words.

1 John has a new pair of brown ....
2 Mr and Mrs Darling go to a dinner ....
3 Everyone sits in front of the .... and listens to the bedtime story.
4 Wendy has got long blond ....
5 Mr and Mrs Darling are very .... without their children.
6 .... has a lot of beautiful parks.

'WE DON'T HAVE MUCH FUN IN LONDON,' SAYS MICHAEL.

We can't count *fun* (uncountable).

• We use *much* for **uncountable nouns**.
  *They have **much** fun in the park.*

We can count *pirates* (countable)
*There are **many** pirates in the forest.*

• We use *many* for **countable nouns**.
  We usually use **much** and **many** in negative sentences, questions or sentences with ***too***.

4 COUNTABLE OR UNCOUNTABLE?
Decide if the noun is countable (C) or uncountable (U). There is an example at the beginning (0).

0	fairy	*C*	5	hair	....
1	water	....	6	milk	....
2	apple	....	7	ticket	....
3	sugar	....	8	music	....
4	noise	....	9	information	....

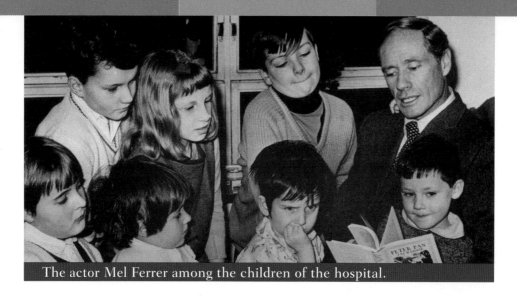
The actor Mel Ferrer among the children of the hospital.

The Great Ormond Street Hospital for Children

In London there is a hospital for sick children called Great Ormond Street Hospital for Children. J. M. Barrie likes children very much. He wants children to be well and happy. He often visits this hospital because he wants to help the children.

Barrie is a kind man. In 1929 he decides that all the money from book sales, films and theatre plays of *Peter Pan* goes to the hospital. And

The entrance of the hospital.

this continues today. This money helps the hospital, the children, the doctors and the nurses.

The children at the hospital can watch the play *Peter Pan* once a year. This is a very happy moment for them.

BEFORE YOU READ

1 VOCABULARY

Match each word with the correct picture.

1 flag
2 skull
3 plank
4 sword
5 prisoners
6 bay

 A

 B

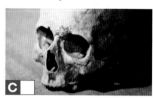 C

 D

 E

 F

2 LISTENING

Listen to the first part of Chapter Six and choose the correct answer – A, B, or C.

1 Where is the *Jolly Roger*?
   A ☐ in the Mermaids' Lagoon.
   B ☐ at Marooners' Rock.
   C ☐ in the bay near Kidd's Creek.

2 What colour is the pirates' flag?
   A ☐ black and white
   B ☐ red
   C ☐ yellow

3 How many pirates does Captain Hook want?
   A ☐ five
   B ☐ two
   C ☐ one

4 Who wants to become a pirate?
   A ☐ Michael
   B ☐ Tootles
   C ☐ John

5 What happens when Captain Hook hears the alarm clock?
   A ☐ He jumps into the sea.
   B ☐ He hides in his cabin.
   C ☐ He wants to fight the crocodile.

CHAPTER SIX

The Pirate Ship

The *Jolly Roger* is a big pirate ship in the bay near Kidd's Creek. On the ship there is a black flag with a white skull on it. It is the pirates' flag. It is night time and there is a yellow moon in the dark sky. Peter sees the children on the pirate ship. They are prisoners[1] of Captain Hook and they are afraid of him. Captain Hook looks at the children and says, 'Peter Pan can't save you now! You're my prisoners!'. He starts to laugh and the other pirates laugh too.

'Smee, come here!' says Captain Hook.

'Yes sir!' says Smee.

'Get the plank ready for these children!' says Captain Hook.

'Alright, sir!' says Smee. He goes to get the long plank.

'What's the plank?' asks John, looking at Wendy.

'Ha, ha!' laughs Captain Hook. 'You don't know what the plank is.

---

1. **Prisoner** : this person is not free.

The Pirate Ship

You must all walk the plank[2] tonight!'

'I don't understand,' says John.

'First you walk the plank and then you fall into the sea,' says Captain Hook. 'And in the sea there's a hungry crocodile. He wants to eat you! Ha, ha'.

'Oh, no!' shout the children. They are afraid.

'But perhaps I can save two of you,' says Captain Hook, looking at the children. 'I want two young pirates. Who wants to be a pirate?'

The Lost Boys look at John. And John looks at Michael and says, 'I don't want to walk the plank. I don't want to be food for that hungry crocodile…'

'What do you mean, John?' asks Michael.

'Well,' says John, 'the life of a pirate is exciting. There are a lot of adventures. Let's be pirates, Michael!'

Michael does not know what to say. He and John look at Wendy.

'That's a terrible idea, John,' says Wendy. 'I'm surprised at you!'

Captain Hook moves his hook in front of their faces and laughs loudly.

'I want an answer from you,' says Captain Hook. 'Do you want to be pirates, yes or no?'

John and Michael look at each other and then say, 'Never!'

'What!' says Captain Hook angrily. 'Then you must walk the plank and die!'

Wendy is afraid. She loves her brothers and the Lost Boys. She has tears in her eyes.

A pirate shouts, 'Who's the first to walk the plank?'

At that moment everyone hears a loud noise. 'Tick! Tock! Tick!! Tock!'

---

2. **Walk the plank** : pirates make their prisoners walk on the long plank and fall into the sea.

'Oh, no! It's the crocodile!' says Captain Hook. 'He wants to eat me!' His face is white and he runs to his cabin[3] and hides there.

'The crocodile is hungry tonight,' says a pirate. 'Someone must walk the plank...'

'Who's the first to walk the plank?' asks Smee, looking at John and Michael. 'Let's go!'

Suddenly Peter Pan arrives, and Tinker Bell follows him. Wendy, John, Michael and the Lost Boys cheer happily. They are very happy to see him.

'Peter's here!' they say. 'He's going to save us!'

Captain Hook comes out of his cabin and sees Peter Pan. He and his pirates are very angry. Hook takes his long sword and says, 'I'm going to fight you, Peter Pan! This is your last fight, because tonight you're going to die!'

Hook fights with his long sword and with his big hook. Peter is very brave and fights with his small sword. He pushes Hook to the back of the ship. It is a terrible fight. John, Michael and the Lost Boys fight the pirates. After a long fight they throw the pirates into the sea.

Peter and Captain Hook fight all over the ship. Their swords make a lot of noise. Suddenly Peter pushes Captain Hook into the sea! Hook shouts, '*Oh, no!*' He falls into the sea and into the mouth of the hungry crocodile. Everyone cheers.

'Oh, Peter!' says Wendy happily. 'You're a very brave boy!' She smiles and kisses him on the cheek.

Peter is happy and says, 'Now the *Jolly Roger* is ours! We can go home!'

'Home!' everyone shouts. 'Let's go!'

3. **Cabin** : (here) a small room on a ship.

48

UNDERSTANDING THE TEXT

1 COMPREHENSION CHECK

Complete the sentences (1-9) with the correct endings (A-I) to make a summary of Chapter Six.

1 ☐ The *Jolly Roger* is
2 ☐ The pirates' flag
3 ☐ Wendy, John, Michael and the Lost Boys
4 ☐ Captain Hook says that
5 ☐ Captain Hook runs to his cabin
6 ☐ Peter Pan and Tinker Bell
7 ☐ Peter Pan is brave and fights Captain Hook
8 ☐ Peter Pan wins the terrible fight
9 ☐ Captain Hook falls into the sea

A   are prisoners of Captain Hook.
B   because he is afraid of the crocodile.
C   is black with a white skull on it.
D   against Captain Hook.
E   in the bay near Kidd's Creek.
F   and into the mouth of the crocodile.
G   with his small sword.
H   want to save the children.
I   the children must walk the plank.

HIS FACE IS WHITE *AND* HE RUNS TO HIS CABIN *AND* HIDES THERE.

In this sentence *and* is a conjunction.

Conjunctions join different ideas in a sentence.

*Come here **and** look at this!*

*They sit in the sun **and** talk **and** laugh.*

*She opens the window **and** looks around.*

2 CONJUNCTIONS

Complete each of the following sentences with one of the conjunctions from the box. You can use the conjunctions more than once.

> or   but   and   because

1   Mr and Mrs Darling are sad .... their children are not at home.
2   'You can choose: you can have an apple .... an orange,' says Wendy to Michael.
3   'I like Neverland,' says Wendy, '................... we must go back to London.'
4   Michael is tired, ... he does not want to go to bed.
5   'You can walk the plank .... you can become a pirate!' says Captain Hook.
6   Wendy cooks .... sews in the underground home.

KEY

3 CONVERSATION

Complete the conversation. What does John say to Wendy? Write the correct letter next to the number. There is an example at the beginning (0).

John: Do you want to go swimming in the Mermaids' Lagoon?
Wendy: (0) ..... *G* ....
John: When can we go?
Wendy: (1) ....
John : At what time?
Wendy: (2) ....
John : Can Michael come with us?
Wendy: (3) ....
John: Why?
Wendy: (4) ....
John: I can teach him.
Wendy: (5) ....

A   Tomorrow afternoon
B   Early
C   At half past two
D   No, he isn't.
E   Because he can't swim.
F   No, he can't.
G   Yes, I do.
H   Alright, then he can come.

CAPTAIN HOOK MOVES HIS HOOK IN FRONT OF THEIR FACES AND LAUGHS LOUDLY.

Loudly is an adverb. It describes how Captain Hook laughs.
We use adverbs to describe **how we do something**.

4 **ADVERBS**
Change the adjectives in the box below to adverbs, and complete the sentences.

| angry | sad | soft | quick | happy | slow |

1 'Peter is going to help us!' the children cry ....
2 'We're late for school!' says Wendy. 'Let's go ....'.
3 John and Michael are tired and they walk ....
4 Wendy speaks .... because the Lost Boys are sleeping.
5 'Where are my children?' asks Mrs Darling ....
6 'I want to fight Peter Pan!' says Captain Hook ....

BEFORE YOU READ

1 **LISTENING**
Listen to Chapter Seven and choose the correct answer – A, B or C.

1 How many empty chairs are there at breakfast?
   A ☐ five   B ☐ two   C ☐ three

2 Who tries to comfort Mrs Darling?
   A ☐ Mr Darling   B ☐ Nana   C ☐ Wendy

3 How many Lost Boys enter the nursery?
   A ☐ six   B ☐ two   C ☐ four

4 Who wants to go back to Neverland?
   A ☐ John and Michael   B ☐ The Lost Boys   C ☐ Peter Pan

5 When can Wendy go to visit Peter Pan?
   A ☐ Next year   B ☐ Every spring   C ☐ In the summer

CHAPTER SEVEN

Back in London

The Darling home in London is a very sad place. Mr and Mrs  Darling never smile or laugh. They always think about Wendy, John and Michael. Every morning at breakfast Mrs Darling looks at the three empty chairs and says, 'Where are my children?' She has tears in her eyes.

Nana goes to the nursery and sees three empty beds. In the evening, Mr Darling comes home after work and he does not hear his children talking and laughing. Mrs Darling often sits in the silent nursery and cries.

She thinks of her children, their games and their happy voices. Nana tries to comfort her, but nothing can make Mrs Darling happy.

She always leaves the nursery window open.

Then one night something wonderful happens. Wendy, John and Michael fly into the nursery! Mrs Darling is sitting near the fireplace and thinking about her children. She hears a voice and turns around.

'Mother, mother!' cries Wendy happily. 'We're home!'

Mrs Darling sees Wendy, John and Michael. She is very surprised. She cannot believe her eyes.

'Oh!' she cries. 'Is this true or is it a dream?'

'Mother,' the children say, 'it's true! We're home!'

They hug [1] their mother and kiss her.

'It's wonderful to see you!' says Mrs Darling, looking at her three children. 'Let me look at you! How wonderful to hear your sweet voices!'

Nana runs into the nursery and barks happily. The children are very pleased to see her.

'I must call your father!' says Mrs Darling. 'George, George! Come to the nursery immediately.'

Mr Darling comes to the nursery and sees his three children. 'This is a wonderful night!' he says happily. 'Our children are finally home!'

'Mother,' says Wendy, 'Peter Pan and the Lost Boys are here too. They're waiting outside.'

'Ask them to come inside,' says Mrs Darling.

The six Lost Boys slowly enter the nursery and look at Mr and Mrs Darling and Nana.

'Mother,' says Wendy, 'these are the Lost Boys. They haven't got a family or a mother. Can they stay with us?'

'Oh, these dear little boys haven't got a family or a mother!' says Mrs Darling. 'Of course they can stay with us. We're their new family!'

'Thank you, Mrs Darling,' say the Lost Boys.

'But where is Peter Pan?' asks Mrs Darling, looking around the nursery.

Peter Pan comes into the nursery and says, 'Here I am! But I don't want to stay here.'

1. **Hug** :

Everyone is surprised and Mrs Darling asks, 'Why don't you want to stay here?'

'I don't want to go to school and learn things,' says Peter. 'I don't want to grow up! I want to be a young boy and have lots of fun forever.'

'But Peter…' says Wendy sadly.

'I must go back to Neverland,' says Peter. 'My home and my friends are there. I'm happy with the Indians and the fairies.'

Wendy is surprised and asks, 'When can I see you, then?'

Mrs Darling thinks for a moment and says, 'I have a good idea. Wendy, you can visit Peter in Neverland every spring! You can stay there for a week.'

'Can I really go to Neverland every spring, Mother?' asks Wendy.

'Of course you can,' says Mrs Darling, smiling.

Peter looks at Mrs Darling and asks, 'Is that a promise?'

'Of course it is!' says Mrs Darling.

'Then I want spring to come quickly,' says Peter happily.

'Yes, very quickly,' says Wendy, laughing.

'Come on, Tink!' says Peter. 'Let's fly home and wait for spring.'

Peter Pan and Tinker Bell fly out of the nursery window into the night sky. They are flying to Neverland!

UNDERSTANDING THE TEXT

1 COMPREHENSION CHECK

Are these sentences 'Right' (A) or 'Wrong' (B)? If there is not enough information to answer (A) or (B), choose 'Doesn't say' (C). There is an example at the beginning (0).

		A	B	C
0	The Darling home is not a happy place.	✓		
1	Mrs Darling is very unhappy without her children.			
2	Wendy, John and Michael fly into the nursery at midnight.			
3	The Lost Boys do not want to stay in London with the Darling family.			
4	Peter Pan does not want to go to school.			
5	Wendy can visit Peter for a week every spring.			
6	Peter Pan returns to Neverland, but Tinker Bell stays in London.			

KEY

2 WRITING

Complete these two letters. Write one word for each space (1-10). There is an example at the beginning (0).

Wendy invites her best friend Elizabeth to her birthday party.

Dear Elizabeth,

My birthday is (0) ....on......... Wednesday. Can (1) ....
come to my birthday party? It starts (2) .... four o'clock in
the afternoon. The party is (3) .... the garden. My mother
(4) .... making a big chocolate cake. There are a lot of fun
games. Bring (5) .... little sister too.

Write to me soon!

Wendy

Dear Wendy,

Thank you (6) .... the invitation to your birthday party. Yes,
(7) .... can come on Wednesday. My little sister cannot come
(8) .... she is ill. Can I bring (9) .... dog, Rover?

See (10) .... on Wednesday!

Bye!

Elizabeth

3 LISTENING

Wendy is taking the Lost Boys on a short tour of London. She is giving them some information about the city. Listen to her and then choose the correct answer below – A, B or C.

1 What is on top of Big Ben?

 A

 B

 C

2 How do Wendy and The Lost Boys travel on the River Thames?

 A

 B

 C

3 What is St Paul's Cathedral?

 A

 B

 C

4 What time do Wendy and the Lost Boys have lunch?

 A

 B

 C

5 Where are they going after lunch?

 A

 B

 C

The dining room.

The Darling Home

What does the Darling home in London look like? It is a comfortable home with a nice garden.

On the ground floor there is a dining room. The family has its meals here. There is a long table with a lot of chairs around it. There are also pictures on the walls.

On the ground floor there is also a large sitting room, with a big sofa and comfortable chairs. People sit here in the evening and read or talk. They also listen to music. Families like singing together. Often someone plays the piano. When friends come to visit, they sit in the sitting room.

At the back of the house there is a big kitchen. Next to the kitchen there is a small room called the scullery. This is where the servants wash up.

The sitting room.

Some big houses have breakfast rooms and libraries.

On the first floor there are the bedrooms, the bathroom and the nursery. The rooms have open fireplaces.

The servants live in rooms at the top of the house.

1 COMPREHENSION CHECK
Complete the sentences (1-6) with the correct endings (A-F).

1 ☐ Outside the house
2 ☐ People have their meals
3 ☐ In the evening the family meets
4 ☐ The scullery is a small room
5 ☐ The bedrooms and the nursery are
6 ☐ There are fireplaces

A in the sitting room.
B next to the kitchen.
C on the first floor.
D there is a nice garden.
E in the dining room.
F in the rooms.

Filmography

The wonderful story of *Peter Pan* is the subject of a lot of films. The first one and maybe the most famous is the cartoon produced by Walt Disney. More recently Steven Spielberg produced **Hook**, with the famous actor Dustin Hoffmann in the role of the cruel captain. The movie **Finding Neverland** is a very original story, that talks about the characters of the story but also about Matthew Barrie.

Title: *Peter Pan*	**Title**: *Hook*	**Title**: *Finding Neverland*
Year: 1953	**Year**: 1991	**Year**: 2004
Director: Walt Disney	**Director**: Steven Spielberg	**Director**: Marc Foster
Production: USA	**Actors**: Dustin Hoffmann, Robin Williams, Julia Roberts	**Actors**: Johnny Depp, Kate Winslet, Dustin Hoffmann, Julie Christie
	Production: USA	**Production**: USA

1 Look at the still of Peter Pan and Wendy. Then answer the questions.

A Where is Wendy and what is she doing? ....

B What page of the story does this still refer to? ....

C Write your own caption for this still. ....

2 Look at the still and answer the questions.

A Who is the pirate in the picture with Captain Hook? ....

B Which are his main features? ....

C Write your own caption for this still. ....

3 Look at the still and answer the questions.

A What are the Darling children doing? ....

B Where are they going? ....

C How are the characters feeling? ....

D What page of the story does this still refer to? ....

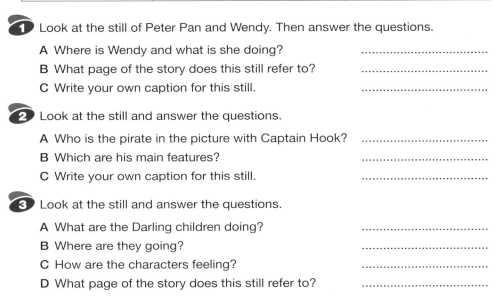

1

2

3

AFTER READING

1 PICTURE SUMMARY

The pictures are not in the right order. Put them in the order they appear in the book.

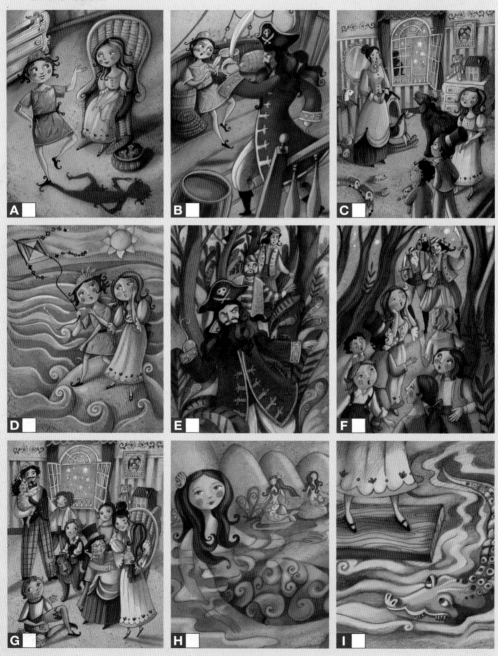

A☐ B☐ C☐

D☐ E☐ F☐

G☐ H☐ I☐

This reader uses the **EXPANSIVE READING** approach, where the text becomes a springboard to improve language skills and to explore historical background, cultural connections and other topics suggested by the text.

The new structures introduced in this step of our **GREEN APPLE** series are listed below. Naturally, structures from lower steps are included too. For a complete list of structures used over all the three steps, see *The Black Cat Guide to Graded Readers*, which is also downloadable at no cost from our website, blackcat-cideb.com.

The vocabulary used at each step is carefully checked against vocabulary lists used for internationally recognised examinations.

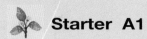 **Starter A1**

Verb tenses
Present Simple
Present Continuous
Future reference: Present Continuous; *going to*;
  Present Simple

Verb forms and patterns
Affirmative, negative, interrogative
Short answers
Imperative: 2nd person; *let's*
Infinitives after some very common verbs (e.g. *want*)
Gerunds (verb + *-ing*) after some very common verbs
  (e.g. *like*, *hate*)

Modal verbs
Can: ability; requests; permission
Would ... like: offers, requests
Shall: suggestions; offers
Must: personal obligation
Have (got) to: external obligation
Need: necessity

Types of clause
Co-ordination: *but*; *and*; *or*; *and then*
Subordination (in the Present Simple or Present
  Continuous) after verbs such as: *to be sure*; *to know*;
  to think; *to believe*; *to hope*, *to say*; *to tell*
Subordination after: *because, when*

Other
Zero, definite and indefinite articles
Possessive 's and s'
Countable and uncountable nouns
Some, any; *much, many, a lot*; *(a) little, (a) few*;
  all, every; etc.
Order of adjectives